D0873237

AN
AGORIST
PRIMER

Books by Samuel Edward Konkin III

Also available from KoPubCo

An Agorist Primer Hardcover 1st Edition
New Libertarian Manifesto
The Legend of Anarcho Claus

Forthcoming from KoPubCo

Rann Gold: Dragon's Bane
CounterEconomics

AN
AGORIST
PRIMER

by

Samuel Edward Konkin III

Paperback 1st printing, November 2009

ISBN 10 0-9777649-7-4
ISBN 13 978-0-9777649-7-6

Published by arrangement with the author.

KoPubCo
publishing division of The Triplanetary Corporation
5942 Edinger Ave., Ste. 113-164
Huntington Beach, California 92649
www.kopubco.com

KOPUBCO and the KoPubCo and Triplanetary colophons are trademarks of the Triplanetary Corporation.

Printed by Lightning Source, Inc.

Cover designed by Black Dawn Graphics

This book is dedicated to
Teny Rule Fisher, Thelma Rule, and
John Fragnito, without whom this book
would not have happened.

Most of all, though, this book
is dedicated to my son,
Samuel Edward Konkin IV,
to whom I offer this blueprint
for liberty as his legacy.

TABLE OF CONTENTS

AN AGORIST PRIMER

PREFACE

Ideas evolve and grow. At some point, an idea connects with so many other concepts that it becomes central to a way of thinking — an ideology.

At some state of an ideology's life, between its birth and death, it reaches a level of maturity such that someone is motivated to divert his efforts from expanding it outward and upward and begins to look downward. That is, the theoretician pauses to pass on the knowledge to those *not* specializing in theoretical development. Perhaps the theoretician is reminded for whom he developed the ideology in the first place.

Agorism is a way of thinking about the world around you, a method of understanding *why* things work the way they do, how they do, and how they can be dealt with — how *you* can deal with them.

Agorism was meant to improve the lot of everyone, not a chosen elite or unwashed underclass. Hence an introductory work that presents ideas without going through the long intellectual history and conflict of competing ideas that produced them. As the creator of agorism, it is most incumbent on me first to attempt to reduce it to basic intelligibility. I hope my efforts find some small reward.

— *Samuel Edward Konkin III*

PUBLISHER'S NOTE

Samuel Edward Konkin III wrote *An Agorist Primer* in 1986. A small number of Xerox copies were circulated to investors in the hope that they would finance the publication of a high-quality, hardcover edition. Though some money was raised, it proved insufficient to produce the book. Even though the photocopies bore text reading "First Edition", it was meant to refer to the proposed hardback edition. That edition, first published in 2008, was the true first edition as SEK3 intended it. This paperback edition was created from the same file as the hardback.

An effort has been made to update the book in order to keep it relevant, though none of the timeless — and timely — agorist philosophy has been altered. Such archaic terms as "videotapes" and "cassettes" have been replaced by "DVDs" and "downloads". Information about major wars since 1986 have been added, staying — we hope — in the spirit of SEK3's other analyses. Notice has been taken of the collapse of Communism, brought about in no small part by Counter-Economics.

Any mistakes, failures to catch archaisms, or errors of analysis added to the original text are entirely the fault of the current editor and not of the late author.   — *V.K.*

INTRODUCTION

Agorism can be defined simply: it is thought and action consistent with freedom. The moment one deals with "thinking," "acting," "consistency," and especially "freedom," things get more and more complex.

Hold on to the virtue of consistency. The refusal to compromise, to deceive oneself, to "sell out" or to "be realistic" created agorism. Consider "being realistic." This usually implies that theory is fine for thinking, but in practice one must deal with reality. Agorists believe that any theory which does not describe reality is either useless or a deliberate attempt by intellectuals to defraud non-specialists.

When someone urges you to be realistic, may you pick an agorist book to get the best description you can find of how agorism actually works. If you want to find books and articles that will "fake reality" for wishes, whims, fears, and spite, look for labels such as "Liberal," "Conservative," "Socialist," "Communist," "Fascist," or — worst of all — "middle of the road" and "moderate."

Reality knows no moderation; it *is* — all the way.

One way of thinking came close to agorism and is fairly well-known today; we will deal with Libertarianism later in some detail. An ideology of Liberty, it had to choose at one point between consistency with reality and being the "politics of liberty." It chose the latter: the contradiction of seeking political power over others to eliminate political power over others.

Those who continued to seek liberty consistently and without the practical contradiction of Libertarians became agorists. This is a second, historical definition for you.

Agorism is an ideology, then, but it is also a scientific and definitely materialist way of thinking. It is not a religious view — save that it believes absolute freedom to be moral — nor does it wish to displace anyone's religious views — unless they lead to slavery. Agorism wants no "true believers" in the sense of blind followers. Like any scientifically based mode of thought, it will evolve as does our understanding of reality. One who has faith in something proven false that was once a tenet of agorism is not an agorist.

Reality is our standard. Nature is our lawgiver.

In a general sense, agorism is scientific in that it bases itself on verifiable observations about reality. But it is scientific in a specific sense as well. It may be hard for chemists, physicists, and engineers to believe that a "hard science" was ever developed in fields such as economics and political science; but the discovery of this science by me — a hard-bitten theoretical chemist, cynical of "soft" science — led eventually through libertarianism to agorism.

An Agorist Primer

The study of human action (*praxeology*)* produced some repeatable observations deserving the title of scientific law. The area of human action dealing with exchanges between acting humans (*catallactics*)* covers the same area of thought that economics is supposed to cover, but often with very different conclusions.

This kind of economics (sometimes called Austrian economics)* was used by speculators such as Harry Browne and Doug Casey for investing in hard-money instruments, beating taxes, and surviving when society around them is operating on unreason and folly. It is that potent, a tool for survival amidst gloom and doom.

However, it can be more. By applying this economic understanding to all human action regardless of the wishes, whims, fears, and spite of the most powerful agency in society — the State (coercive government) — a new field of theory dealing only with practical action emerges: Counter-Economics.

Finally, when libertarian theory meets Counter-Economics, what comes out — in strict consistency, both external and internal — is Agorism. This is still another definition.

And this is the definition with which I feel most comfortable, the one that the thieves of the intellect find hardest to pervert or steal: *Agorism*

---

*If this area of study appeals to you, by all means go to the source: *Human Action* by Ludwig Von Mises. You'll find all the terms starred herein are derived and defined in detail.

*is the consistent integration of libertarian theory
with counter-economic practice; an agorist is one
who acts consistently for freedom and in freedom.*

A basic understanding of agorism falls naturally into four phases of integration or four steps of learning. In addition to grasping the premises involved, one should be able to apply them. Remember always that agorism integrates theory and practice. Theory without practice is game-playing; taken seriously, it leads to withdrawal from reality, mysticism, and insanity. Practice without theory is robotic; taken seriously, it leads to tilling barren soil and showing up for work at closed factories. Perhaps it would help to think of theory as wedded to practice where divorce leads to ruin. Or the relationship could be viewed as that between brain and stomach or mind and body: neither can survive without the other.

So four concepts and four applications lead naturally to eight chapters.

The author and publisher welcome your questions because they will indicate where we can clarify and improve subsequent editions.

Chapter One
ECONOMICS

Economics is a dismal science. Those understanding certain economic concepts profit flamboyantly. Economics is a tool corporations and governments use to control society. Those understanding economic concepts have toppled governments that refuse to face the very same concepts. Economics is a meaningless college exercise. Speculators understanding economics make millions of dollars and save others from financial ruin. Here is our problem: all the above statements are true.

If that makes you think there's an inconsistency in the use of Economics, you are correct. With a lower-case "e," economics is the study of relations between people involving goods and services. With a capital "E," Economics is an institution financed mostly by government and its tax-privileged foundations. With foundation money, this institution controls — however imperfectly — those who would learn and teach economics at government schools or private colleges.

Maybe this appears to be a big deal made out of little; after all, is not most of chemistry and astronomy and mathematics also institutionalized? Imagine the case where only "pro-government chemistry," "conservative astronomy," or "socialist biology" was taught and those who tried to teach *straight science* were vilified as crackpots. Fantastic? Lysenko's pseudo-biology was taught in the Soviet Union because it was more in line with Marxist theory than was straight genetics. Currently, Man-Made Global Warming is approaching the status of state-approved climatology, with dissenters shouted down, de-funded, smeared as apologists for polluters, and even threatened with the recision of their academic degrees.

Perhaps you will grant that government can use its control of schools and colleges to teach a twisted version of economics. Could, then, better economics be taught if government were improved? The answer is, "not a chance!" As you will see in Chapter Six, if people understood economics, coercive government could not survive. (And uncoercive government is a contradiction in terms.)

What we wish to accomplish in this chapter is simply to give you a basic understanding of real economics. No, this is not just to help explain the rest of this book; with even an elementary understanding of economics, fewer con games can defraud you — especially the high stakes, political kind.

Let us start with *why* people act economically.

Value

Right down there at the very bottom, we be-gin. Human beings act. Why? Ludwig Von Mises said it best: to remove felt unease. If you were perfectly content, nothing and no one nagging at you, and you knew that if you did nothing you could continue to be content, would you move? Remember, moving from this state would increase unhappiness. Of course you wouldn't move. Even if you said you would move to relieve boredom, you would be violating the hypothesis. You would be *more* bored by moving since that is an increase in unhappiness.

Aha! Is that not a contradiction? you rightfully ask. Correct. And if an assumption leads to a con-tradiction, it is wrong. Our assumption was that you could achieve a state of ease; therefore, such a human condition is impossible.

In reality, man always has reason to feel unease: to feed himself, clothe himself, shelter himself, reproduce, and feed, shelter, and clothe others, amuse himself, and so on. Unease cannot be elimi-nated. It can, however, be reduced. It can also, unfortunately, be augmented.

If you seek to starve yourself or bore yourself, you increase your unease. Some actions you per-form achieve negative goals; some achieve positive ones. Those which remove felt unease are *values*.

If someone else has something that will remove your unease but taking it will increase theirs, we have a conflict in values. This conflict in values need not arise from direct confrontation. Suppose you and another are offered a scrumptious dessert, and the other is dieting desperately. You value it; the other disvalues it.

Value is subjective. This simple insight, made by Carl Menger (teacher of Von Mises), revolutionized primitive economics and cured many of the problems plaguing the science since Adam Smith.

Had Marx heeded Menger, socialism would have been abandoned.

Subjective value leads to individualism. It also explains so powerfully why people trade and it demolishes theories of "exploitation". Before subjective value, Marx could look at the work of Adam Smith — who thought value arose from the amount of labor one put into producing something — and see no productive role for anyone but laborers, concluding that all the others must be parasites. There *are* parasites in our system, economics tells us, and we shall use our new understanding to ferret them out in the next chapter.

Finally, when people trade, they are acting to remove felt unease in both directions. You may give up a smaller value for a larger but never the other way around — voluntarily. If you're willing to let your brother work for you and pay him "more than he's worth," you know that this means, to you, "he's worth extra because he's my brother." You've still gained a greater value.

If values were *not* subjective, why would anyone trade? We would all value things equally and be content with what we had. Well, not entirely; we could also want *more* of a value. Onward, then, to the next powerful economic concept.

Marginal Utility

Suppose you, being a shepherd, had ten sheep, and a nice woolen coat you laboriously made from your eleventh sheep. If someone came along and offered you a coat just like it for your tenth sheep, you'd tell them to buzz off. Along comes a rich shepherd and sees your coat. You tell him how you got it and even tell him how to make one. He can think of better things to do than to make a coat, but he'd like to have one. He'll trade you a sheep for a coat.

No better off subjectively, you refuse. He offers you two and you know you'd be ahead: you can make another coat and have eleven sheep again. Meanwhile, the rich shepherd would rather have 98 sheep and a coat than a hundred sheep and no coat.

But this example so far is still one of subjective value. His final offer is three sheep. Joyfully, you accept. As you are leaving, you run into another poor shepherd with ten sheep and a coat. (There seems to be a lot of this going on.)

He offers you coat for sheep and is willing to accept two sheep. You're still ahead — eleven sheep *and* the coat! And you don't have to make it yourself. Such a deal!

Using the wool coat as our *medium of exchange*, we find out something interesting. Sheep are sheep (as far as this example is concerned) yet while you traded your eleventh sheep for a coat and would not have traded your tenth, you did trade both your twelfth and thirteenth sheep for a coat. This principle where you value each additional unit less and less is called *marginal utility*. (You are operating at the *margin* and "*utility*" is an older word for value.)

All sheep (and dollars) are not alike; marginal ones are cheaper. Besides giving us an idea which can handle *more* in economics, and also help us to spot frauds such as tax redistribution (see next chapter), marginal utility leads directly to the next concept.

Division of Labor

Subjective value may lead us to think we would prefer producing some goods rather than others, or transporting them, trading them, serving them, or storing them. Yet it is marginal utility which tells us why this specialization works. If I produce ten cooked hamburgers an hour and you produce twelve, and we happen to eat the same, it is obvious who has more surplus to trade and will be eager to do so. I should check out other lines of productivity or move to a less desirable (at least to *you*) location where I can compete.

This process, where we are led to specialize by greater productivity and greater reward (value-seeking), is called *division of labor*. Von Mises speculated that it was the glue holding society together; and if you think of society as bigger than a nuclear or extended family, he is right.

If Jane sings beautifully, and we do not, *division of labor* is why *I'm* writing this book, eating *your* hamburgers, and *we're* listening to Jane on the radio.

Basics

With such basic ideas as those about trade, exchange, goods and services that you (hopefully) already brought with you to this discussion, added on to the concepts of subjective value, marginal utility, and division of labor, you are properly armed for understanding agorism. There is far more to economics and still more being discovered and written about by the (all too few) right kind of economists.

Before moving on, there is one economic specialty that deserves some extra attention. Since it is so much on everyone's minds, you probably guessed that it is *money*.

Money

Money is heavily mystified and it's not hard to see why. "A fool and his money are soon parted" is a truism nearly as old as money itself. If you can be confused as to what money is or how it works, you can be parted from it by those who know what money is.

Remember our sheep example? We called the wool coat a *medium of exchange* to show the different values of a sheep. But if we had many wool coats and one sheep being traded back and forth, we could use the same example to show the marginal utility of the eleventh coat (or whatever number happened to work) and the use of sheep as a medium of exchange.

Straight trade of goods for goods — barter — is crude, and problems related to making change are difficult to solve. Sheep die and wool coats wear out; they do not store value well. And — since value is subjective — changes in your needs, tastes, and circumstances alter your values anyway. Nothing can store a changing quantity or, as math majors would say, fix a variable.

What we would like is something that makes change, stores its value, and is universally acceptable (everyone wants it all the time). To be blunt, there is no such thing and never will be, though all bank directors, congressmen, and commissars might decree otherwise. *Subjective value* assures us of that.

But suppose some substance could be divided down to its atoms without changing, be more resistant to wear and corrosion than almost anything else, be easily recognized and easily checked as to purity, and be valued already by a lot of people for its usefulness and good looks. Suppose further that it "did it better" than anything else offered in competition?

Would not most people flock to it and *make it money*? No laws would need be passed or institutions founded or advertising campaigns conducted to make it so. Nature would take care of it. Second, third, and fourth choices might be used, but the first would be the *standard* by which the others were measured.

Such a substance has been known for millennia. Gold, and its close chemical relatives platinum, silver, and copper, remains the choice of a free market. Even in an *unfree* market, where money is imposed by force against the will of traders (that is, by *fiat*), gold remains the money of the "underground economy" and of the "overseas economy" working around the *fiat money*.

Why fiat money exists at all and what it has to do with inflation is an important topic in our next chapter.

Value-Free Economics

So far we have avoided loaded terms such as "free market," "competitive economy," "free trade," "fair trade," and so on. The Austrian economists (Menger, von Mises, Eugen von Böhm-Bawerk and their students) believed economics should be a science free of such terms, a "value-free" (*wertfrei*) science.

Science has values; try to engage in research without a commitment to truth or an affinity for reality. Many people hold values that are impossible to achieve in reality and are frustrated — they hurt themselves. Many people seek to gain values by misrepresenting reality to others; when they are challenged, they accuse the exposers of holding different, competing values. Thus "value-free scientists" — including economists — find they cannot remain forever neutral in their ivory towers.

To the extent, though, that they try by keeping their own subjective values out of the way, they do accomplish much. The scientific method works. And being able to tell people that stealing from everyone and then giving it back to them will make them less well off is useful, not matter how unpopular.

This is where the *application* of economics enters.

Chapter Two
APPLIED ECONOMICS

Agorism is more than economics, but agorist thinking is impossible without that basic understanding. Just applying the basic economics we have learned so far can sweep away a lot of misconceptions and eliminate a lot of confusion about how the world works. We also can deal with some of the misleading con jobs of Economics — however, explaining why Economics is so twisted will have to wait until we apply libertarianism later.

The Free Market

Agorism upholds the free market. To understand why, one first needs to know what the free market is and what its alternatives are. Again, *why* is left for later. The term "agorism" is derived from the ancient Greek word *agora*, meaning an open market place.

The market is not a single place or center. Goods and services are exchanged at the corner store, on the stock exchange, at a swap meet, in your backyard, or across the Internet. Playing a game with a friend is not a market transaction, but foregoing the time that each of you could spend on working or buying or selling is a market transaction.

All social interaction has a market component. Economics may be far more pervasive than we thought. It is difficult to imagine how we could have a free society — should we wish it — without a free market. Perhaps we should be clear with reference to what we mean by "free."

Free means the absence of coercion. Coercion is threatening violence upon someone in order to make him surrender something. In a strictly value-free sense, then, coercive human action offers to create a greater *disvalue* to you if you do not yield up your lesser value. You gain nothing but lose less.

Repeated application of coercion destroys values. The coercer gains without producing anything of value and the victim always loses. Voluntary exchange, as we have seen, occurs when both feel a gain in subjective value. Unease is relieved in both directions. In coercive transactions, unease is increased.

Retrieving your goods from the coercer with the threat of greater force and enough extra for your time and trouble at least wipes out your loss, although it leaves the original coercer with a net loss. At this point, he may finally become aware of the value destruction of coercion. Or he may simply decide he needs still greater force. (The biggest force of all in an area is usually the State, but we'll come to that later.)

Strictly speaking, the free market is the absence of all that coercion. If there were only a few "private thieves" and they were usually apprehended and forced to make restitution, something very close to a free market would exist. People would have locks, fences, alarms, and insurance policies and protection-agent policies, but would act otherwise on the assumption that they were free to give up their property to those of their choice and accept from others who gave freely to them. They could not plan on people changing their minds, but they could make contracts (exchanging a good here and now for one to be given later) so that if others changed their minds, some compensation would result.

Planning and Chaos

It quickly becomes clear that planning is far more practical in a free market than in a coerced market. If coercion becomes regular and predictable, innovative people find ways around it and soon enough join forces to evade the coercive regulations, frustrating and/or starving the coercer. (See the next chapter.)

So new forms of coercion must be brought in and economic planning is disrupted once again.

Some argue that a free market is Chaos; they see no one giving orders and so think that there is no order. In reality, a completely free market is a highly decentralized order. Each "cog" in the great machine keeps itself well-oiled and seeks to mesh itself with the other cogs in ever-better fits. An even better example is the human body. While the brain has some overall direction, it cannot instruct various cells to go about their ways delivering blood and building tissue and contracting muscle and transmitting energy. A disease or parasite may "direct" some cells to a common task — but this results in disruption of the natural order. Even without a "foreign invader," if the brain could force some cells to act other than naturally, the entire body would suffer by this imposed order and the body could die.

The fallacy in "planned economics" is the error of assuming that order is *imposed*. Scientists are aware that order is something you look for in nature — it's already there.

Economics tells us that attempts to impose order by coercion are destructive and chaotic, yet "economic planning" of the imposing kind is common to nearly all schools of Economics. We begin to see where the gap between economics and Economics lies.

Competition and Monopoly

It's nice if more than one person offers to trade the same thing with you. You usually can get a better deal. When more than one seller offers identical goods, and when more than one buyer offers to acquire the same goods, *pure competition* exists.

If only one buyer or seller is available, the buyer or seller is said to have a *monopoly*.

Competition is always good in the sense that it

maximizes value exchanges. Although it would take more theory to prove this, most people have had enough experience to accept the foregoing as a factual statement.

Surely not all monopoly is bad? If we banned all monopoly, then Leonardo da Vinci would have had to give up painting what only he can paint. And the Beatles would have had to stop composing what only they can compose. In fact, since a little bit of "artistry" distinguishes all goods, pure competition is impossible. There are no identical products.

Yet, for your subjective purposes, you can see no difference *worth paying for* among all sorts of goods. And they do not have to be all that similar. With fifteen dollars you might decide to buy a book you wished to spend the evening with. Finding the book sold, you consider a movie instead. The lines are too long, so you buy a six pack instead and go home.

Someone else would have different goods competing for that fifteen dollars, even if he had started out trying to buy that same book.

If I told you at this point that some Economists defined a "free market" as a "perfectly competitive" market, you might wonder when they lost their senses. After all, if people want to produce different things (remember division of labor), and are more productive doing so, you will not get "perfect competition" in the free market. You will have lots of competition by giving each human actor maximum freedom to explore his values and find alternatives.

Now if I tell you that these Economists say that

if a market is not "perfectly competitive," force should be used to make it so. You probably are beginning to wonder if I have not lost my senses. Whatever these Economists are after, it is not a free market. Nor will they generate any gains since values are always net-destroyed by coercion.

Adam Smith defined monopoly as a grant of exclusive trading by the king. It was a royal privilege; that is, the State coerced some people not to produce goods when the king's friend was already doing so. Breaking up these *forced monopolies* was an issue for freedom-lovers and rightfully so.

The problems arose when people stopped thinking clearly — or had their thoughts muddled by Economists. *Monopoly* became bad, not because it was coercive, but because it was not competitive. Clear thinking and consistency lead us easily to realize that the opposite of *forced monopoly* and of *forced competition* is *natural monopoly* and *free competition*. The correct opposition is the coerced market *vs.* the free market.

Cartels

One problem with monopoly we seemed to have overlooked: do not the "big get bigger" and the "small get driven out" even if the market is left alone? The answer is obvious empirically: historically, it has never happened. There is extensive literature by the better sort of economists on many historical examples where businesses were accused of forming "trusts" — that is, attempting to monopolize one industry through *cartels*.

Most cases, when State trustbusters were brought in to "break up" a large company, proved to have been instigated by smaller companies against a more efficient competitor.

Cartels, as Dr. Murray Rothbard has beautifully shown, tend to break up from market forces. The most efficient cartel member can outsell his fellow members and has a tremendous incentive to "cheat" on the cartel agreement. He can "steal" the customers from his fellow members and soon does, "under the table." Upon discovery, his fellow cartel members fight back by cutting prices and the cartel disintegrates.

In a coerced market, however, the cartel will run to someone to force compliance with the cartel. That someone is, in any realistic unfree market, the State. And once again we are back to the *forced* or *State monopoly*.

Profit and Enterprise

Sometimes the terms "free enterprise" and "capitalism" are used to mean "free market." *Capitalism* means the ideology (ism) of capital or capitalists. Before Marx came along, the pure free-marketeer Thomas Hodgskin had already used the term capitalism as a pejorative; capitalists were trying to use coercion — the State — to restrict the market. Capitalism, then, does not describe a free market but a form of statism (see Chapter Five), like communism.

Free enterprise can only exist in a free market

and is an acceptable synonym, yet while the term *market* covers all human transactions, *enterprise* seems limited to certain types of business. And what about *profit*? Is it the result of "exploitation," enterprise, hard work, or something else?

Applying economic knowledge here resolves the problem clearly but it will take a little effort to follow through. According to (Austrian) economics, there are three productive functions in the marketplace: *Labor*, *capital*, and *entrepreneurship*. In the simplest, primitive economy, *capital* consists of tools, food you have stored to keep you going until your harvest comes in or you can sell the shoes you made, and storefronts or wagons to take your goods to market. *Labor* is the work you put into farming or shoemaking or whatever.

Entrepreneurship is direction, the reins of the operation, deciding where to invest the capital and which and how many workers to hire. As the market progresses to greater wealth and complexity, we can see that the important components of entrepreneurship are *risk-taking* and *innovation*. Speculators, inventors, and artists (without patrons) are the best-known, fairly "pure" entrepreneurs. They take risks, create (1) a product that did not exist before, which turns out to have a demand; (2) a better product to replace one that existed before, winning away the demand; (3) a cheaper method of producing or marketing the same product, again winning away the demand.

The *gain* resulting from pure entrepreneurship is *profit*. It is *not* the everyday *return on investment* that a businessman counts over his expenses and takes home.

Windfall profits occur when there is a sudden change in market conditions, such as weather wiping out crops or producing bumper harvests, mineral and oil strikes suddenly coming onto the market or — when the market is not free — sudden government interference in the marketplace. Those who make the most effort to anticipate the unexpected tend to make the most profits.

Taking risks also means one can introduce products no one wants, invent devices that are laughed away, and create artsy trash. Such creations incur negative profit (*loss*) and, alas, this is at least as common, historically, as profit.

Nonetheless, without entrepreneurship — *enterprise* — the economy would stagnate as people continue investing the same capital in the same way, over and over, and workers continue at the same jobs. When skilled laborers begin to die out and capital runs out of components, such as minerals at mines or new forests for timber, the economy would *regress* and collapse.

Everyone is part laborer, pan capitalist, and part entrepreneur, but by division of labor we tend to specialize. There is nothing to prevent us from all being wealthy (some day, at any rate) and using our money (as James Garner put it so well in the film *The Wheeler Dealers*) as a way of keeping score in capital investment. And capital, in the form of ever-more-intelligent computers, can reduce labor to a vestigial activity (as necessary as the human appendix). Entrepreneurship, on the other hand, is increased, not decreased, by a progressive market. As our society becomes more complex and more wealthy, more people will specialize in entrepreneurial activity and more people must be free to do so.

Entrepreneurship cannot be forced. When bureaucrats "plan," they spend their time finding ways of covering their posteriors and pass the losses on to the taxpayers. They fear replacement and since they reap little or no reward for success, they become timid about actually taking risks, and spend their time creating red tape entanglements designed to stymie innovation.

Regulation

There is nothing positive to say about regulation. Regulation is coercion. It prevents subjective values from being satisfied, "protecting" only those who do not wish to be protected and penalizing only the law-abiding. Regulation destroys initiative and stifles innovation. Regulation stagnates markets. Regulation can and does kill people when the regulators deny victims the right to take a chance with so-called risky medication.

Regulation is motivated by fear, envy, and colossal ignorance. There is nothing that can protect innocent people more than a thorough education and a vigorous pursuit of fraud; yet regulation of advertising and experimentation destroys information transfer and regulation of quality merely certifies incompetent "professionals" and protects *them* from fraud charges.

If all the regulation passed in any country you wish to name were completely obeyed, let alone enforced, we would all be dead.

Consider a particularly pathological case in the United States of America. If you charge a price for your product higher than your competitors, this is taken as evidence under the Sherman Anti-Trust Act that you have a monopoly and charges may be brought against you. The same problem arises if you charge the same; that is considered evidence of a cartel and you and your competitors can all be fined. Finally, if you charge less than your competitors, you are violating the "Fair Trade" laws in most states and can be arrested and fined. It is impossible to obey all the regulations.

Taxation

There is a serious moral question about taxation that we will leave for later. Let it suffice now to recognize that taxation takes something from someone against his or her will and is a violation of his or her subjective values. Any specific form of taxation directs resources counter-entrepreneurially. In short, taxation has no place in a free market.

Interest

There are three very closely related concepts in economics, and they have to do with *capital*, *land*, and *money*. It is often said that capital earns a *rate of return on investment* (remember, only entrepreneurs make profits), land earns *rent*, and money earns *interest*. With an efficient medium of exchange, an entrepreneur will quickly shift from capital goods of one type to another if the rate of return is higher in one sector of the market than the other. Land is a fixed form of capital, and — if we are in a free market — we should expect rent to come to equal the rate of return as in other investments — assuming no risks (where profit would be added or subtracted). And so it is with interest.

Originary interest is what money earns if you lend it out to an entrepreneur risk-free. Should you accept risk yourself, you may add on a *risk component*, a form of profit. At the same level of risk, in a highly developed market, interest rates should stabilize and slowly decrease — as wealth increases.

Only if something becomes powerful enough — coercive enough — to monopolize (by force) all the media of exchange (or *money supply*) and then increase it so that the value of each unit declines, will another component appear to increase the interest rate (regardless of risk). Conceivably it could decrease the money supply so that the value would be expected to increase and interest to be discounted. In an extreme case, this *inflationary component* could drive interest rates to zero or negative — that is, someone pays you to take his money and give it back to him later. *Deflation* is rare, as there is very little incentive for controllers of the money supply to deflate.

Inflation

Understanding how inflation works and what to do about it made the fortunes of the "gold bugs" and investment analysts mentioned earlier. While there is considerable fog and confusion thrown around this subject, inflation is simple enough to understand if you follow our step-by-step logic and (always!) watch for inconsistencies.

From Chapter One we know what money is. Free-market money could be affected by, say, a gold strike or, if for some reason the gold was all kept in a "Fort Knox," by James Bond's Goldfinger nuking it. Even then, there would be a brief dip or jump in the "price of gold" (the price of money is simply the inverse of the prices of everything bought with it), and stability would resume at the new level. In a worldwide market, the effect — even of nuking Fort Knox — would be barely noticeable.

Inflation is the increase of the money supply. Inflation results only when the most powerful force in society — the State — commands a monopolistic fiat money system, creates *legal tender* laws (legal tender compels the monopoly, contracts are not upheld in other "tender" or money), and — with army and police to back it up — debases a form of money that was acceptable in the marketplace.

States that have imposed fiat money from scratch (such as in newly emerging Third World countries) find their money rapidly rejected in favor of foreign currency and gold. The usual route to inflation takes four steps: **1)** Replacement of money by *certificates* for the money. A weight of gold or silver is replaced by a certificate claiming an ounce of gold or pound of silver in some precious metal warehouse or "bank." **2)** *Legal* definition of possession of the certificate as equivalent to possessing the wealth. (The government gets into the act.) **3)** *Restriction* of all exchanges (save primitive bartering) to the legal certificates; this is the creation of legal tender. **4)** *Issuing* certificates without money to back them up. At this point we have fiat money and inflation.

Inflation leads to crack-up booms (German in 1923) and depressions (U.S. in 1929). This analysis is a bit more complicated and is best left to the more cataclysmic scenarios we'll present near the end of the book.

Oh, and as you probably guessed, one result of inflation is a general rise in price level. Notice that some prices rise faster than others, and some even seem to drop. Only the distortion is common to all price changes.

A Little Knowledge

If you have mastered the first two chapters, congratulations! You will quickly discover two things by simply reading your daily newspaper or news blog or shooting the breeze with your acquaintances.

First, you will discover the appalling level of ignorance with which most of society is afflicted. Be careful — some people get very irritable when challenged by someone who knows what he is talking about. A knowledgeable person might be tempted to use his knowledge to bilk the ignorant. Many people with only a little knowledge do just that. However, there are moral ways to profit by your understanding and, by all means, go to it.

Second, you will discover that the appalling web of Statism is controlling — or attempting to control — nearly every aspect of human action. You will probably feel smothered and that is not surprising. You may also feel like giving up and giving in — but survival alone dictates otherwise.

Survival — let alone prosperity — demands that you tear through the web of *legislation* and follow nature's *laws* instead. You must abandon Economics to the regulators and the political "businessmen" who play ball with them. You are left with the alternative: stifle yourself and starve or embrace Counter-Economics.

Samuel Edward Konkin III

Chapter Three
COUNTER-ECONOMICS

We see that nearly every action is regulated, taxed, prohibited, or subsidized. Much of this Statism — for it is only the State that wields such power — is so contradictory that little ever gets done. If you cannot obey the (State's) laws and charge less than, more than, or the same as your competitor, what do you do? You go out of business or you break the law. Suppose paying your taxes would drive you out of business? You go out of business — or you break the law.

Government laws have no intrinsic relationship with right and wrong or good and evil. Historically, most people knew that the royal edicts were for the king's good, not theirs. People went along with the king because the alternative looked worse. This line of thinking leads to Chapter Five, so we'll just note here that even today, society recognizes the *conscientious objector*: the religious dissenter to laws that his deity forbids him to obey, the man or woman who follows the Law of God or Nature against the monopoly of force in society. Since they would rather die than submit, a society which restrains its government from heavy repression will exempt many objectors.

But everyone is a resister to the extent that he survives in a society where laws control everything and give contradictory orders. *All (non-coercive) human action committed in defiance of the State constitutes the Counter-Economy.* (For ease of later analysis, we exclude murder and theft, which are done with the disapproval of the State. Since taxation and war encompass nearly all cases of theft and murder, the few independent acts really should be classified as other forms of statism.) Since anything the State does not licence or approve of is forbidden or prohibited, there are no third possibilities.

A *Counter-Economist* is (1) anyone practicing a counter-economic act; (2) one who studies such acts. *Counter-Economics* is the (1) practice (2) study of counter-economic acts.

The Size of the Counter-Economy

The Counter-Economy is vast. Our brief study of economics tells us that this should be no surprise. The more controls and taxation a State imposes on its people, the more they will evade and defy them. Since the United States is one of the *less* (officially) controlled countries, and the Counter-Economy here is fairly large, the global Counter-Economy should be expected to be even larger — and it is.

U.S. government estimates of the size of just the tax-dodging part of the Counter-Economy is twenty to forty million of the population. The

Western European Counter-Economy is larger; in Italy, much of the civil service sits in government offices during the early part of the day and then moonlights at private jobs and business in the afternoon and evening.

Communism collapsed in no small part due to the Counter-Economy. Nearly everything was available in the Counter-Economy with only shoddy goods and shortages in the official socialist economy. The Soviets called Counter-Economic goods "left-hand" or *nalevo* and entire manufacturing assembly lines co-existed *nalevo* with the desultory State industry ones, on the same factory floor. Counter-Economic "capitalists" sold shares in their companies and vacationed in Black Sea resorts. Managers of collective farms who needed a tractor replaced in a hurry look to the Counter-Economy rather than see their *kolkhoz* collapse awaiting a State tractor delivery. Currently, the Russian government seeks to reestablish State control of the economy by granting monopolies to cronies and imprisoning recalcitrant corporate executives. As with Communism, this flirtation with Fascism is just as doomed to failure.

Nothing works in "right-hand" communism; everything works in the left-hand free market.

From "black" market apartments in the Netherlands to "black" housing in Argentina, the Counter-Economy is well known to the people of the world as the place to get things otherwise unobtainable — or keep things one has earned. Inflation breeds flight from fiat money; exchange controls have created dual exchange rates in nearly every country on the globe. Whatever the number of local currency units a tourist can get for his dollars at the official exchange rate, he or she can get more on the black market.

Smuggling is so commonplace that nearly all tourists slip purchases past customs agents without thinking. Perhaps 20%-30% of Americans fail to report taxable income (actually nearly 100% fail to report at least some); but, in Latin American countries, close to 80% goes uncollected and the State supports itself by ever-greater inflation of the fiat money supply.

The border between Hong Kong and Communist China and even the ocean straits between Taiwan and the mainland bustle with illegal trade. Western DVDs and jeans were once illegally available in most provinces of China — now they're manufacturing them there!

Saigon, renamed Ho Chi Minh City, remains the black market center of Vietnam. Even more telling, it produces most of the goods and services of all Vietnam. Myanmar's (Burma's) rigidly controlled official economy, according to the *Manchester Guardian*, is nothing but paper and the entire market has gone black.

Under the noses of American forces, Afghani tribes grow, process, and ship heroin by the metric tonne.

Tax evasion, inflation avoidance, smuggling, free production, and illegal distribution still compose only half the Counter-Economy. Labor flows as freely as capital, as hordes of "illegal aliens" pour across borders from more-statist to less-statist economic regions.

Consciousness-altering substances and even unproven medicines such as dichloroacetate and Laetrile make up a well-known but small fraction of the Counter-Economy. Drugs are grown on huge plantations, refined in scores of factories and laboratories, distributed by fleets of boats, planes, trucks and cars, and sold to customers by regiments of wholesalers and armies of street dealers.

The State's imposition of some people's moral codes on others leads to Bible smuggling in atheist States and pornography publishing in conservative religious States. The "world's oldest profession," as sexual prostitution has been titled, is also — if that title is true — the world's oldest counter-economic industry.

Feminists seeking control of their own bodies look to the Counter-Economy to obtain contraceptives and find midwives to deliver babies *their* way in the Counter-Economy.

Nobody works at anything anywhere which is not connected with Counter-Economics. Those looking for a more exhaustive listing of counter-economic activities, with all the sources and references footnoted, are invited to read the author's upcoming book *Counter-Economics*.

Information

Two Counter-Economic industries are singled out for their importance to agorism. Justice is a commodity; its manner of distribution defines a social system and will be covered in detail in Chapter Seven.

The other business is Information. The Internet explosion has led the American State — for now, at any rate — to throw up its tentacles at regulation of the Information industry. Every legislative session, however, brings new attempts to tax and control the World Wide Web. But consider this well: should the Counter-Economy lick the information problem, it would virtually eliminate the risk it incurs under the State's threat. That is, if you can advertise your products, reach your consumers and accept payment (a form of information), all outside the detection capabilities of the State, what enforcement of control would be left?

At the leading edge of Web development today is *encryption*. Advanced researchers have developed methods of "locking away" data in memory banks that defy any "breaking in." That is, the State cannot reach the invoices, inventory lists, accounts and so on of the Counter-Economist. An area of human society immune to the power of the State deserves the name — if anything does — of Anarchy. The State, though, continues to attempt to penetrate privacy with quantum computing methods of cracking even the most complex cryptographic schemes. Will the Counter-Economy respond with quantum cryptography? Stay tuned — the race is hardly at an end.

This leads us to two crucial questions: what happens if the State is abolished and we have a free market and why has the Counter-Economy not overwhelmed the existing economy already? These questions bring us back to the land of theory where libertarianism answers the first question and agorism the second.

Before we deal with them, let us consider some applications of counter-economic business practices and social interactions, which will both illustrate our descriptions and possibly be of some profit to you and yours.

Chapter Four
APPLIED
COUNTER-ECONOMICS

Counter-Economics is application. People have discovered and acted in a Counter-Economic way without understanding what they are doing, why they are doing it, and even denying that they are doing it at all.

Understanding what you are doing usually helps, and applying Counter-Economics systematically and consistently maximizes both your profit and freedom. As it turns out, the basic formula is no more difficult than simple accounting arithmetic used in all business.

The basic law of Counter-Economics is to trade risk for profit. Having done so, one naturally (acting to remove felt unease) attempts to reduce the risks. If you reduce your risks while others continue to face the higher risks, you naturally out-compete and survive longer. And you profit.

What's The Risk?

It is possible to make a reasonable estimate of the risks you are taking in Counter-Economic activity, which is better precision than many business ventures offer. The government itself gathers statistics concerning apprehension of "criminals." And publishes them. The police agencies brag about how few cases are solved and how fast the "crime rate" is growing to justify ever-bigger budgets.

Nonetheless, most "crimes" go completely unreported and undetected, so the State's stats are an upper limit of apprehension. That is, their figures are useful as maximum risk. The highest apprehension rate for the most foul crimes seldom hit 20%, an indication of government effectiveness in maintaining public order.

Is It Worth It?

Suppose you wish to do something Counter-Economic. To be specific, you can buy something for $10,000 and sell it for $20,000. Your regular overhead is $5000. Your net return on investment is $5000 (on an investment of $15,000 that's 33%, extremely high) but, since there is a risk, how can you tell if the return is worth it?

Let's say the government claims it catches 20% of those doing what you want to do. If you are caught, the penalty would be a (maximum) fine of $50,000 or six months in jail. Your "downside" risk, then, is 20% of $50,000 or $10,000. In this example, it would *not* be worth it: to gain $5000 but risk losing $10,000.

If the apprehension rate were 10% and the fine $25,000, then your risk would be $2500 for a gain of $5000. As is obvious, you could get caught one time in ten, pay off your fines, and still come out way ahead. Of course, all these calculations make certain assumptions about your subjective values. You may fear risk to a pathological state and any risk is too much. Or you may love frustrating the State and take high risks for lower gain just for the fun of it.

Actually, a more realistic risk estimate would include the price of a lawyer to beat your charges and the probability of being convicted after apprehension.

Assume that the retainer to your lawyer raises your overhead $1000 per transaction. Now your payoff is $4000, but the conviction rate (with plea bargaining and court delays) is only 20%. (Again, that is high in many jurisdictions; many cases are dropped long before they come to trial.)

Now your risk, using our first figures, is 20% of 20% of $50,000, or $2000. With a payoff of $4000, a loss of $2000 would deter few entrepreneurs. If you would like a simple formula for your own business, try this:

Counter-Economic Payoff = profit minus loss =
(Promised price) minus (cost minus overhead) minus
((Penalty or Fine) x (probability of arrest) x (probability of conviction))

If positive, go. If negative, don't go.

Lowering Risks

Taking reasonable steps to conceal your activities from accidental discovery, learning to talk only to trusted friends, spotting poor risks or government agents all reduce your risk and increase your payoff. As you develop techniques to lower your risk, you will increase your counter-economic activities. More of them become profitable.

These side effects include the creation of an agorist society. More on that in Chapter Seven.

Counter-Economizing

While it's true that you cannot obey all the inconsistent laws of the State and so be completely "white market," you can live completely Counter-Economically and be completely "black market."

In the middle 1970s, the federal State passed a regulation imposing a maximum speed limit on U.S. highways of 55 mph. With the threat of cutting federal funds to states and counties, the entire driving population decelerated to a creeping crawl. Or did it?

Consider the following calculation: at 55 mph a trucker can drive 55 miles in an hour, 550 miles in ten hours and 2200 miles in 40 hours. At an average of 70 mph, he makes 700 miles in ten hours and 2800 miles in 40 hours.

To make it even clearer, assume that the trucker nets $1000, after costs, for each 600 mile run.

He makes four runs legally for $4000 in an easy week, or $5000 by extending his hours or working weekends. At 70 mph he makes $5000 for the (roughly) 40 hour week.

With that type of incentive, the race went to the swift and the "double nickel" speed limit was scofflawed. But being caught and fined could wipe out that advantage. Suppose fuel were consumed at a rate that cost an extra $200 at the higher speed, and you received an average fine of $200. Four busts a week and it's no longer worth it.

Along came Citizen's Band Radio. Put $200 or $400 once into a CB radio investment, reduce your busts to once a week, and you're back in business. And that, of course, is what happened. Truckers "spotted" for each other, formed convoys, and thwarted the State's "Smokey Bear" highwaymen.

Consider the side effects:

- Truckers found "solidarity" economically, culturally, and anti-politically
- A CB culture exploded into the popular culture with C. W. McCall's classic song "Convoy"
- Non-truckers who were willing to buy a CB and learn the culture (especially the language) were accepted freely into the ordered highway anarchy. More evasion of regulations followed and the Counter-Economy grew
- Truckers, many of conservative upbringing, became considerably more tolerant and willing to help other "lawbreakers" when their common enemy, Smokey, threatened.

The CB explosion is not meant here to be a model, in the sense of waiting around for the State to trigger off mass rebellion by an egregiously stupid law. This happened to be a particularly spectacular case, but no more than the sudden jump in counter-economics when Prohibition was passed in the 1920s or when the draft led to two-year slavery, and possible death, in 1964. And the State does not learn from its mistakes, as recent efforts to reimpose the 55 mph limit as well as reactivate the draft arise again.

Counter-Economizing Yourself

Whatever service you provide the market, you know best how to counter-economize. You know best which regulations to avoid first for maximum payoff-to-risk ratio. You know which suppliers can be trusted and which cannot. You know which customers to trust and which not to trust. Division of labor, subjective value, and human individuality all contribute to making your case (and everyone else's) unique.

If you seek or want advice on how best to counter-economize, you need personal counseling (similar to investment counseling). But, considering the hundreds of millions of people — many with educational and cultural handicaps — who counter-economize quite successfully, the challenge is not that great. You need mostly the will to do it. (And that "Psychological Counter-Economics" will be important as part of Chapter Eight.)

It's undoubtedly easier to extend your counter-economizing when everyone else is doing it. Most people *are*, but in small and different ways.

Still, if you could win more suppliers and customers over to your trust and get them to counter-economize, they would not only resist turning you in but they would develop a tendency not to leak secrets and would, therefore, decrease your risk and increase your payoff both ways.

This fact is the driving force toward expansion of the Counter-Economy. This force is what Agorism unleashes against the State.

Chapter Five
LIBERTARIANISM

The basic premise of agorist thinking is that Counter-Economics has failed to free society because Counter-Economics lacks a moral structure that only a full-blown philosophical system can provide. In this chapter, we deal with the other half of this problem: an ideology unconnected to reality. Where Counter-Economics is application without theory, Libertarianism is theory without application.

Many Gods, One Morality

Libertarianism differs from all other philosophies by its *pluralism*. It does not to ask how you came to the fundamental moral premise: religious revelation, atheistic observation, natural law theory, or many others. Christians, Taoists, Objectivists, and Pagans travel different routes to arrive at one moral code in common: *initiation of coercion, or the threat of violence, is immoral.* This is the libertarian principle.

Two things follow from the phrasing: (1) there are no exceptions, hence libertarianism affects all human action by this formulation; (2) it is phrased *negatively*, so that anything else is permissible human behavior, though each adherent may find other acts immoral or objectionable.

Christianity yields a yes-no answer to every aspect of human activity; so, too, Marxism, Islam, Objectivism, and many, many other understandings of the world's nature. In these systems, anything not prohibited is mandatory. You *must* or you *must not*. Libertarianism answers only that you *may* or you *may not*, leaving choice to you.

Any religion or ideology that swears not to coerce others to act in accordance with its precepts is compatible with libertarianism. *All* religions and ideologies that use force for anything save self-defence (in the narrow, immediate sense, excluding "preventive aggression" and other such rationalizations) are enemies of libertarianism.

Libertarian Society

Libertarianism's very pluralism prevents one from ascribing any unanimous characteristic to Libertarians. They all want Liberty, but for different reasons, and see different ways of achieving it. Some would take control of the State and "force people to be free," others would not even resort to violence to defend themselves. Giving all those groups their due for enriching Libertarian thought and life with greater variety than any other ideology, the rigorous application of consistency (to which agorists and this book adhere) does settle some issues.

A *free society* is one in which Man is constrained only by unthinking Nature. His fellow men leave him alone. One can personally live up to this and one can admit only those who uphold it, expelling all those who don't. But one cannot prevent anyone from instituting aggression, one can only deal with it after the fact.

Statists advocate creating a bigger criminal, a great monster institution which will terrify nearly everyone, innocent or guilty, into submission. This organization will extract some form of acceptance from its "citizens" and yet plunder them at will (taxation). It will control their behavior and even their thinking, though some statists seek to place some restraints upon this super-criminal organization. Some of those who advocate the strongest restraints (as they perceive them) call themselves "limited government libertarians." Since they seek a small state or "mini"-*archy*, they are *minarchists*.

Consistent libertarians see no place for criminals, even to fight other criminals. They believe free-market (all-voluntary) methods will take care of the few criminals; finding them (investigation), arresting them (delegated protection), trying them (arbitration), and restoring lost value to the victim from the aggressors (restitution). The *means* of accomplishing this vary from communal power to highly technological, competitive business agencies and others in between, such as neighborhood block associations. Such "no-government libertarians" are called *anarchists*. The peaceful libertarians who refuse even to defend themselves have to be classified with anarchists.

It is bitterly ironic that heavy State propaganda has convinced many people that anarchists throw bombs, since most anti-war movements, draft resistance, disarmament, and tax resistance groups were organized by anarchists of one sort or another. Perhaps 0.01 % of those calling themselves anarchists throughout history have used a bomb; 100% of all States bomb, shell, and machine-gun regularly as a matter of course.

A *Libertarian society* is one which approximates a free society save for a small percentage of criminal aggression, which is handled by voluntary mechanisms. A society in which aggression gets "out of hand" is one with a *de facto*, if not *de jure*, State or government: a *statist society*.

Libertarianism and the Free Market

A few libertarians advocate communal or neighborhood social organization with collectively held "property" voluntarily surrendered. Most libertarians have adopted the free market and the economic understanding of it developed in Chapter One. So whenever a conflict between the Economics of government intervention or confiscation (*statism*, for short) and free enterprise emerges in public debate, Libertarians rush to the forefront of defence of the individual or non-state group.

Libertarianism often confuses statists of the Left wing and the Right by opposing both. Libertarians see war as total "socialism" and march with many Leftists against it. Yet opposition to welfare statism allies Libertarianism with some Rightists.

But Statists of the Left and Right are easily distinguishable from libertarians in any coalition: threaten the State's existence and observe their reaction.

Conservatives will give up free enterprise rather than see government abolished; liberals will go to war rather than see government abolished. Libertarians will abolish the State and end both socialism and war.

Libertarianism and the Counter-Economy

Libertarian dissidents, from Polish professors to American students, make up an intellectual field of Counter-Economics. A Yugoslavian theorist, raised in the Marxist tradition, called for removing politics from Socialism and embracing a market economy.

It would appear that there is a natural affinity between the philosophers of freedom and the practitioners of Counter-Economics. Indeed, few libertarians would deny the moral correctness of the latter. An early slogan some radical libertarians put on a button was "Defend The Black Market." Libertarianism in the United States traces its history from the Abolitionist movement to free the slaves, an act of human counter-economics.

And yet, while many abolitionists created and maintained an Underground Railway to assist slaves who freed themselves counter-economically, others called for upholding the law, working within the system and engaging in politics to take over the government and pass laws to free slaves. The same division between activists and reformers afflicts modern libertarians — and many other ideological movements, to be sure.

George Orwell, who came to a type of libertarianism from activism in the Socialist movement of the 1930s, castigated some of his fellow socialists for refusing to dirty their hands in actually fighting for their beliefs on the battlefields of Spain. This perceptive author of *1984* and *Animal Farm* noted these hypocritical dilettantes' proclivity for hanging around English drawing rooms and waxing eloquent for the socialist cause while contributing precious little else. He called them "Parlor Pinks."

Libertarianism is afflicted with more than its share of "Library Libs" today. Some, though, are horribly paralyzed by the question, "*How* do we achieve a free society?"

This combination of strategic paralysis, moral lassitude, honest confusion due to the rich variety of libertarian pluralism, and not a little "selling out", has weakened libertarianism to the point where what is presently called the "Libertarian Movement" may no longer be trusted to defend the Counter-Economy and achieve a libertarian society.

The next chapter shows why.

Chapter Six
APPLIED LIBERTARIANISM

A Brief History of Liberty

The history of the Libertarian movement can be divided into four historical periods. The first covered most of our history, when many men and women derived the ideas of freedom and defended freedom as they understood it with little comprehension of the mechanics of human action. Some of these, such as the Quakers of Pennsylvania, settled colonies away from predatory statism and developed peace and trade with the natives.

The American Revolution erupted the year that Adam Smith published the first basic work on economics. Still, the confused American Revolutionaries allowed the Federalist statists to restore a strong central government by a bit of trickery called the "Constitution," a piece of paper which supposedly guaranteed to restrain the new State. Most of the Revolutionaries — nearly all the signers of the Declaration of Independence, for instance — opposed the Constitution. Many Americans were taken in by the statist selling job and laid down their arms that were defending them, practically in exchange for the paper guarantee. As soon as the new government was elected, it sent the military to Pennsylvania to crush the tax-rebels who opposed the new tax on whiskey distillation.

In England, soon after, a man named William Godwin took the political ideas of the American Revolutionaries to their logical conclusion and became the first anarchist. In the 1830s European intellectual scene, a man named Max Stirner combined anarchy with defence of the free market (as far as Adam Smith understood it then) and created a philosophy of egoism or total individualism. For a time, he contested with Marx and Engels for the loyalty of the Young Hegelians in the German clubs. They wrote a two-volume defense of their theory against Stirner (*The German Ideology*).

In the United States, Josiah Warren continued the anarchist tradition in Massachusetts. One of his abolitionist followers, Lysander Spooner, finally developed the killing argument against the U.S. State in his remarkable natural law treatise, *No Treason: The Constitution of No Authority*. Alas, it was nearly a century late because the State was entrenched well enough to fight a civil war to destroy the remaining internal restraints on its power — naturally, under the pretext of expanding freedom by abolishing slavery.

Spooner saw through that smokescreen and supported *both* abolition *and* secession of the

Southern States. His follower, Benjamin Tucker, discovered Stirner's European individualism and combined the two traditions. The heyday of Individualist Anarchism, during the publication of Tucker's *Liberty* magazine, from 1881 to 1908, could be called the second stage of Libertarianism. George Bernard Shaw, for example, broke into the American literary scene through Liberty. (The full title of Tucker's journal was *Liberty: the Mother, Not the Daughter, of Order*.)

Tucker still had problems with economics, not understanding subjective value or the validity of rent, interest, and profit. While willing to accept anything arrived at freely, he and his associates spent their energies on side issues and invalid controversies. When World War I broke out, they lost the center stage of history to the socialists for half a century.

At the same time that Tucker himself was giving up, brilliant Austrian economist Ludwig Von Mises wrote his doctoral thesis (1910), *The Theory of Money and Credit*, which explained interest, inflation, and business cycles. His analysis led to an easy explanation (and prediction) of the Great Depression, but it went unheeded. In 1949, Mises published his *magnum opus, Human Action*. Along the way, he sent the Communist Economists into a panic by proving that economic calculation was impossible once socialist statists destroyed the free-market pricing system.

During the 1920s and 1930s, proto-libertarians such as H.L. Mencken and Albert J. Nock kept the philosophy alive but in despair. One of Nock's students, Frank Chodorov, reached one of Mises's students, Murray Rothbard. In 1950, Rothbard connected with the American anarchist tradition and the modern libertarian stage began.

Another of Nock's students, Suzanne LaFollette, inspired many modern libertarian feminists. More women — Rose Wilder Lane and Isabel Patterson — kept libertarianism alive in the 1940s.

For twenty years, Rothbard tirelessly sold his consistent libertarian view in intellectual circles and was purged from the Right, from Objectivists, from the Left, and various other groups, always taking a few more with him, never despairing. In 1969, during the heat of the student revolt against the Vietnam War and the draft, both the leftist Students for a Democratic Society and the rightist Young Americans for Freedom split internally. The anarchists from SDS joined the free marketeers from YAF at a convention called by Dr. Rothbard, and thousands of young activists were unleashed onto the campuses to fight for pure freedom.

Within a few years, there were a million Libertarians in North America and small groups from England to Spain to Australia. Libertarians graduated and started businesses or entered the higher levels of academy, bringing reinforcements to Dr. Rothbard and his previously small corps. Libertarian reporters, authors, and even newscasters spread through the media.

Robert LeFevre, another libertarian educator contemporary with Rothbard, graduated hundreds of businessmen from his seminars and thousands from Rampart College. Leonard Read and his crew reached many from all walks of life at the Foundation for Economic Education. New foundations and institutes sprang up.

Early in 1971, a group of Californians started a "Libertarian Party" as a front for distribution of literature and appeal for equal time on local media. In December of 1971, David F. Nolan convened a founding convention of a Libertarian Party in deadly earnest. Rothbard scoffed at the idea of a party as wildly premature.

In 1972, an LP presidential candidate got few votes, but, thanks to a renegade Republican elector from Virginia, John Hospers, Professor of Philosophy at the University of Southern California, received one electoral vote. His running mate, Toni Nathan of Oregon, became the first woman to receive one. The elector, Roger MacBride, became the LP nominee for president in 1976.

The LP emerged from two sources: impatience and inconsistency. In 1972, the student movement collapsed but the graduates needed years to affect society by working their way through the system and building alternatives outside it. This desire to achieve results *now* — get rich quick — was expressed in the return of many who had rejected the Statist system to re-enter it, though most of those entering the LP were not the politically cynical old-timers.

The more raw recruits to libertarianism had little direct experience with politics and so accepted arguments that the party would spread the word to people used to receiving it via the biennial electoral process. While half the LP recruiters swore that the LP was an educational tool and would never win an election and take power, the other half promised the replacement of the Republicans by the new party and the transformation of society from the top down.

During 1973, the party threat became serious and the libertarian movement began to split. The anti-party libertarians called themselves various names such as New Libertarians, Left (more consistently radical) Libertarians, Radical Libertarians, and exotic names such as Voluntaryists. The common goal of these activists was to deflect the Party anti-principle in the minds and hearts of most libertarians and pursue the original goals of Liberty in libertarian — that is, anti-political — ways. The *Partyarchs* (as those who professed being ruled by a party, yet called themselves anarchists, were then called) and their minarchist allies were small in number but did have an advantage in getting newspaper and television coverage. (Radical libertarian campaigns such as the 1976 "Vote For Nobody" CounterCampaign received publicity on several hundred radio stations and 50% of registered American voters failed to cast ballots.)

More and more "pure" libertarians gave up on the label as the word was increasingly identified with a group out to take political power — as opposed to abolishing it. The New Libertarians found that many who would agree to live freely and trade without aggression were repelled by the Libertarian name.

Finally, in 1983, the Movement of the Libertarian Left, the New Libertarian Alliance, and others moved to drop the Libertarian label entirely. Some chose the name Voluntaryism. Those wishing to promote the completely consistent ideology described in this book chose the name agorist.

During the 1973 struggle, the challenges for an alternative strategy to politics were answered by the NLA founder who discovered and coined the term Counter-Economics (see Chapter Three). In 1980, the NLA published *New Libertarian Manifesto*, which explained agorism and beyond to libertarian activists.

The Libertarian Failure

Libertarians were and still are a pluralistic group. Different interpretations of Liberty and how to achieve it were cheerfully tolerated for the most part. The appearance of a "Party line" was anathema to this spirit of living variety. The burning issue shifted from "which new libertarian theory works and which does not?" to "which 'Libertarian' candidate can get elected?"

To many, Libertarianism was a fine theory which had no obvious practice. There are many paths to freedom (true) and each individual should choose the one he or she thought most workable. One that was chosen swallowed up the others.

(How it did was simple: it tied into the State's grant of monopoly to ideologies that form a centralized "political party" and then spokespersons of that ideology are automatically represented as servitors or functionaries of that party, *even when they vigorously deny any connection*, by the statist media.)

And, then again, maybe not. "Libertarian" may have come to mean "LP member" but agorists, Voluntaryists, Left Libertarians, and such still outnumber the few thousand LP members and even the never-since-matched million votes their candidate, Edward Clark, received in the 1980 U.S. presidential race.

Whether or not libertarianism failed and died — perverted — so near to 1984 (Orwell's deadline for tyranny's triumph... in the form of an all-powerful *party*) or was simply a stage in the evolution of agorism, building a theory to explain and morally defend Counter-Economics, is a moot point. Both positions are, in a sense, true. Agorism is here and viable for those who wish to live as freely as possible now and increase their freedom in the future. What now calls itself "Libertarian" cannot honestly offer that anymore. Those who understand this will reject the "Libertarian" Party and other political solutions to the statist problem; those who accept the LP will waste their time, energy and wealth in building a new means of keeping people in bondage under the thumb of the State.

The Libertarian Insight and Fallacy

Libertarian theory provided the crucial insight as to why Counter-Economics was morally correct as well as (obviously) practical and very profitable. The crucial issue was that of the State, its nature, and its evolution.

The easiest paradigm (short model) for the origin of the State was offered by Franz Oppen-heimer, a German sociologist, and adapted into American libertarianism in Albert J. Nock's 1935 book, *Our Enemy, The State.* All historical examples fit this simple paradigm:

When most of humanity settled into peaceful farming communities, with perhaps larger marketplaces (remember the original *agora* of Greece) in towns, some people discovered a means of surviving parasitically from the productivity of others. They formed robber bands and attacked towns and settlements, plundering, raping, and murdering. Probably the original barbarian hordes were hunters who took to hunting man when their game died out rather than taking to farming, trading, or productive manufacture.

These roving groups were a small minority (or their victims would have died out and they as well) but large as compared to a single town or village. Somewhere along the way, one of them discovered that they could allow the peasants to live with enough to survive on and come back at the next harvest for another raid.

Then these raiders had another idea: they would stay in the same towns, steal lightly but regularly, murder enough to keep the peasants and merchants in line, and live well. Other areas, seeing these petty kingdoms arise, decided to submit themselves to their own home-grown warlords so that they would not fall prey to foreign warriors. (*The Book of Samuel* in the Old Testament describes the anarchist prophet Samuel trying to convince the Israelites that they didn't really want a king but finally giving in to them.)

Parasites must remain a minority or kill their hosts. So they discovered religion (and later ideology) as a means to intimidate peasants and win the all-important *sanction of the victim* (an apt phrase of Ayn Rand's). Brutal thugs became "kings by divine right" and some very powerful statists called Emperors, Pharaohs, or Tsars were said to *be* divine, the unstoppable choice of gods.

And so these barbarian raiders institutionalized plunder (taxation), murder (execution and warfare), and even rape (*droit de seigneur*, for example). They took control of roads to plunder the caravans (tolls, tariffs), they suppressed all rival criminal gangs with their own (police), and established their own churches, schools, judges, and even philosophers, minstrels, and artists to work in their royal courts.

Thus was born the State.

As people come to understand this situation, and especially important questions of conscience split religions and ideologies, dissidence grew.

The State learned to survive by adapting. It used its Court thinkers (intellectuals) to come up with new ways of mystifying the people.

The kings "limited" themselves and shared their plunder with aristocrats and certain favored merchants. Thus was born mercantilism (which Adam Smith challenged). Then even peasants and workers were permitted to plunder their fellow merchants, farmers, and workers. This was called Democracy. Groups were allowed to organize to fight over who should steal from whom (though an elite of bureaucrats and very rich businessmen continue, no matter who is elected) and thus were formed political parties.

The libertarian analysis superbly explained the political history of the world and — combined with free-market economics — analyzed depressions, modern warfare, and revolutions, describing their causes and predicting the futility of political solutions.

When Libertarianism began to organize itself, though, much of the movement was bought off with yet another political party.

To understand the Libertarian fallacy, consider its insight in other terms. Oppenheimer and Nock pointed out that there were only two ways to acquire wealth (food, shelter, tools, entertainment). One could produce some and trade for others — or one could steal those produced. Those are all the choices there are. They named the productive way, the *economic means*, and the parasitic way, the *political means*.

Murray Rothbard, following Ludwig Von Mises's *Human Action* with his own economic treatise *Man, Economy and State*, added that insight onto Austrian economics in the final chapters. The demand for elucidation was so great that he wrote, in detail, an entire book on the subject: *Power and Market*.

It is amazing that, for a time, even Dr. Rothbard forgot his own lesson. The choice was power/politics *vs.* market/economics. Using political means to achieve free-market ends is self-destructive and self-defeating.

The recognition of the Libertarian incompatibility of statist means to anti-statist ends was the first *agorist* insight. Following that, the new agorists looked for the proper means to achieve a free society or at least a fully libertarian society. They sought market means only.

The author of this book and his companions found the Counter-Economy "staring them in the face" as soon as they thought of looking.

Chapter Seven
AGORISM

To understand agorism fully and to compare it to competing ways of thinking, one needs to know two things about it: its goal and its path to that goal. This knowledge is critical to evaluating all ideologies. The goal is *living in the agora* and the path is *expanding Counter-Economics*. Remember our constant, if not nagging, emphasis on consistency, both internally and with reality. Agorism *must* have a path consistent with its goal and a goal consistent with its path.

The Axioms of Agorism

A free society is the goal of many people, not all of them agorists or even libertarians. Agorists can see nothing but a free market in a free society; after all, who or what will *prevent* it?

The First Axiom of Agorism: *the closest approach to a free society is an uncorrupted agora (open marketplace).*

An axiom is a principle or premise of a way of thinking. It is arrived at by insight, induction, and observation of nature. Theorems are arrived at deductively from axioms. A **"zeroeth" axiom of agorism** might be *"there are no contradictions in reality and theory must be consistent with reality."* Commonly known axioms in philosophy are "existence exists" and "A is A." Well-known mathematical axioms are "things equal to another thing are equal to each other" and "a statement leading to a contradiction with a theorem or axiom is false."

The first six chapters of this "primer" preceded the actual presentation of agorism to give you, the reader, enough understanding of economics, Counter-Economics, and libertarianism to see from where the insights that produced agorism were derived. They were not chosen arbitrarily but rather as a result of years of bitter experience and, in some cases, furious battles and acts of resistance. The "hard core" agorists had to have something worth dying for, and, far more important, worth living for.

The Second Axiom of Agorism: *the agora self-corrects for small perturbations of corruption.*

This axiom leads us to a far more detailed picture of what our nearly free society would look like. It means simply that free-market entities will defend the free market. *People* have to choose to do it, of course, but the incentive (offering of subjective-value satisfaction) will be present to motivate them to do so and will be sufficient to motivate enough people to do so. Occasional criminals will be discovered, sought, found, apprehended, tried, sentenced, compelled to deliver restitution, and (if possible) deterred from further actions.

The Third Axiom of Agorism: *the moral system of any agora is compatible with pure libertarianism.*

This axiom means that life and property are safe from all those who act morally in this society. We will describe this in the next section. But let us complete the axioms first.

The Fourth Axiom of Agorism: *agora in part is agora in whole; to a workable approximation, the corruption of an agora raises protection costs and risks.*

This axiom's use will become blindingly clear when we deal with the path.

Agorism has more theory, but it is derived from these axioms. For the professional logicians tripping across the theory for the first time, I need to add a **fifth axiom** for completion: *agorism* **qua** *theory is an open system.* This simply means that we may discover and add on other axioms, then check to see how consistent they are with what we already have.

The Goal of Agora

With that short burst of hard philosophy in the last section, we are ready to picture the society we are aiming for. The goal of agorism is the agora. The society of the open marketplace as near to untainted by theft, assault, and fraud as can be humanly attained is as close to a free society as can be achieved. And a free society is the only one in which each and every one of us can satisfy his or her subjective values without crushing others' values by violence and coercion.

It's a bit late to notice, perhaps, but if your highest values *require* murder and theft, you will not like the agora. Still, you have not wasted your time as you have just read an introduction to the thinking of your worst enemy.

Science fiction has given us many convincing portrayals of future societies, from the grotesquely tyrannical (*1984*) to the transitional-to-freedom (*The Moon Is A Harsh Mistress, Kings of the High Frontier*) to actual free-market anarchies that accidentally arose (*The Syndic, The Great Explosion, The Probability Broach*). One even portrayed a likely scenario for an agorist revolution (*Alongside Night*)!

Still, we cannot predict or foresee all the changes. Fortunately, we can get a good picture of an agorist society by picking out those changes (from our present statist societies) that must occur (or we simply don't have agorism). Our axioms give us that much.

States will be gone. Roads will be run by competing market companies and kept in repair (for a change) to attract more customers. Then, again, cars may levitate over the roads for all we know or fly or take tunnels to preserve scenery. If you can think of one good reason to do something some way, in a free market it will be tried and many ways will work at the same time for different reasons.

The post office will be gone and mail — if not replaced by e-mail entirely — will be efficiently and cheaply delivered ever-faster.

War will be gone. "Defence budgets" will be gone. Taxes will be gone. You will pay for what you get only when you want it — unless what you want is a gift.

I repeat, and cannot emphasize enough or wax floridly enough: the opportunities in freedom explode into the unimaginable. The sheer complexity of all possible choice moves to the infinite as restrictions approach zero.

Let us focus very narrowly on only one business in the totally free marketplace.

Justice

Justice is a business. It's not free; someone must pay for its workings. While *Justice* in the abstract is not an economic question (remember the *wertfrei* of Chapter One), the *obtaining of justice* is an economic service.

Consider this illustration: Your completely tricked-out media center is stolen from your home. You notify Laissez Faire Insurance & Protection Company immediately. As fast as modern technology permits, you receive an identical screen, receiver, game station, speakers, cables, and a sack full of remotes to replace the original, with downloads of any programs you missed in the interim. You have achieved *full restoration* of your subjective value to the condition it would have been had there been no act of aggression. Surely that is the goal of Justice.

Now, how is this paid for in a free market, consistently with our understanding of economics and libertarian morality? The moral position first: you delegate LFI&PCo as your *agent* to use *defensive* force to regain your missing property and all expenses incurred. (If LFI&PCo attempt to extract more from the ultimately caught thief, they're on their own. The *thief's* Insurance and Protection Company is entitled to defend the thief.)

Costs are paid for in three ways. First, as *insurance*: a small number of criminals may elude even the highly efficient, super-technological, extremely competitive protection agencies of the agorist future. Insurance is simply sharing the risk of something happening with all the others subscribing to LFI&PCo. As the odds of a thief "getting away with it" approach zero, your premium approaches zero. Second, as *protection*: you install locks and detectors, alarms, and maybe even booby traps. Actually, since your premiums will go down as you make yourself aggression-proof, protection will incur minimal additional costs. Third, as *restitution*: the aggressor, when apprehended, pays LFI&PCo (1) the cost of replacement of the purloined or damaged goods; (2) interest for the time the goods were stolen; (3) any costs related to apprehension, including fees for investigators, arresting agents, arbitrators (market judges), and, if still necessary, enforcers' charges to reclaim your property.

Note all the differences between statism and agorism. First, in a State, you can expect nothing from the police if you report a criminal. Maybe, some day, you'll get your property back if the criminal is ever caught and when they're through using the components as evidence. Since the odds of police accomplishing this are less than 10%, your insurance premiums (if the government still allows insurance companies) reflect the sharing of the high risk of theft *plus* whatever taxes the State tacks on *plus* the inefficiencies and additional costs of government regulation of the insurance industry. Did you ever try to collect insurance? Notice the form-filling and red tape — just like any other *government* bureaucracy imposed on a supposedly free enterprise?

Second, in a State, you are under the control of the State in a criminal proceeding — even though you are the victim! You will be told when to appear, where to go, and you will be forced to see the case through even if *you* change *your* mind. In the agora, should the matter go to arbitration, you will be required to report your loss since you want it replaced. That's all. The theft may even have been recorded on video, but even if not, the protection company's detectives do all the work. You stand back (or go about your business) and let them do their jobs. That's all. You may never be called again even if the thief is caught, convicted, and compelled to provide restitution. If LFI&PCo needs more testimony from you, they will *ask* you to attend the arbitration and, if they err, *they* will pay for the error. Should they need you inordinately, they will pay you for your trouble — or they will let you go and lose the case if you want too much for your time.

Third, in a State everything is monopolized; your appeal is to another judge who works for the State, too. In the agora, competition and choice is everywhere. There are plenty of insurance and protection companies from which to choose, all eager for *your* business. They can choose from a number of crack detectives, all competing to show that they are the best investigators. Should the matter go to arbitration, a number of arbitrators are competing for the positions, hoping to prove themselves the fairest and most worthy of your company's hire.

Furthermore, if crime risks go up in your neighborhood, it is in the interest of your protection company (and those companies of your neighbors) to hire protectors (or guards) to patrol your area. Unless you attack your neighbor, their protectors will never threaten *you*.

Fourth, in a State, your police protection is just as likely to arrest you for some crime that has no victim. There are no such victimless "crimes" in the agora.

Fifth, the rights of the victim (you) can never be overridden by the rights of the real criminal. Under agorist justice, the arbitrator rules on the evidence that you are, or are not, entitled to restitution of goods (or even parts of the body, as technology makes that possible), interest for time lost, and your protection agency's expenses, including detection and apprehension costs. The moment the line is crossed into extracting *more* from the media-center thief than full restoration of your components and all costs incurred, you or your company become the aggressor and the ex-thief's protection agency will now honor its contract to defend him. (All insurance and protection contracts in an agorist society will stipulate that you cannot be protected from restoration proceedings after the protection company has defended you up to a fair arbitration. This ideal, seldom lived up to by States, is called "due process.")

The difference between agorist protection and State policing has many more characteristics but this list gives you a good idea. There is nothing the State can offer you in moral protection that the market cannot offer; and the free market will function faster and better than the State. It's true that an occasional market company may be unsound, but you will always have the option of switching to a better competitor. Under a State, you *know* your protection service will always be the same — poor with no alternative.

The State offers one thing the free market cannot and will not offer: *aggression*. If you wish to attack your immediate neighbors, you'll need State police to attack them for the crimes of belonging to the "wrong" religious group or of taking the "wrong" intoxicant or of performing sex in a way of which you disapprove. And, of course, your neighbors will need State police to attack you for similar "reasons." If you want to attack faraway neighbors, you need a State army.

Or maybe you want to live in peace and freedom and will be satisfied with protection and defence.

Two Words or So About National Defence

Full agorism obviously needs no "national defence." There are no nations to defend and no nations from which to be defended. Local protection against occasional criminals is sufficient.

Once in a while, criminals might band together to overwhelm a single protection company. Then the agorist protection agency merely needs to hire another protection company to assist it.

Similarly, should one protection company "go bad," a few of the hundreds of others would be enough to apprehend its agents and shut it down. But, in fact, market forces would sap such a company's destructive power long before it came to that. People raised in an agorist society would stop paying its insurance premiums and shift to its competitors. Detective and investigation agencies would terminate their contracts with it. Arbitrators would consistently rule against its aggressive moves. Agents working for the company would quit and go elsewhere. Secretaries and office help would walk out rather than have their reputations sullied by associating with such un-agorist types. Even restaurants and grocery stores would refuse to sell to the renegades or would hike their prices to show their additional loss of subjective value in dealing with such coercive filth.

Perhaps the company-turning-State would pay higher prices to hold on to their employees and supplies or replace them. But where would they get their money? They would *lose* customers the moment they started to act like a government. It is just as likely that they would collapse if they attempted to live by stealing (tax-collecting) since they would be compelled by force (of other companies) to cease and desist their aggression against those companies' clients.

People raised and educated to love an agorist society could not fall for taxpaying. And if they ever do, we will sink all the way down the road of corruption and oppression to the level of statism... that we "enjoy" today!

The second word about territorial defence deals with the concerns of most people when they meet some version of anarchy — even the businesslike, efficient, free-market kind. How does the non-state defend itself against all the States still left?

The glib answer is "let me count the ways." A few should suffice to allay nameless fears.

First, the context must not be forgotten. Government will not disappear until it is rejected by the overwhelming majority of the people under its rule. It is highly unlikely that other people, in other countries around the world, will be unaffected should North America oust its State through this libertarian infection. A Libertarian International formed in 1980, had its first convention in Zürich in August, 1982, and continues into the 21st century as the International Society for

Individual Liberty. Many of these members could be relied upon to act as fifth columnists in their home countries to stop their governments from attacking the obviously peaceful anarchy.

Second, although we do not rule out "naked aggression," remember that wars are caused by both sides. There is an entire branch of libertarian theory we skipped in making this presentation (actually, more than one) called Revisionist History, which rips the mask off government war propaganda to reveal the gleaming skull underneath. The United States, for example, has not been involved in a single war since the first Revolution that could not have been avoided nor one that would have cost American citizens their liberty had it been avoided (said liberty, to be sure, which they were already losing to their own government). Several volumes have been written about each of these wars, from Establishment and Revisionist perspectives, but, let me just list the bold, simple conclusions here and you can research for yourself whether I'm right.

War of 1812 — US "Warhawks" sought a land grab in Canada. **Pretext** for the war: "impressment of American seamen" in ships running the British blockade of Napoleon. (True but trivial in comparison to war and its cost in lives and freedom.)

Mexican War — U.S. Southern interests sought land grab of Texas and other Mexican territories to form more "slave states" to balance off new Northern "free" states. **Pretext:** Mexico attacked Republic of Texas and thus U.S. soil. (Probably not; and Texas was *not* U.S. soil then.)

War Between The States — North wished to enslave the South; South (justifiably) wished to be free of the North. **Pretext:** Abolition of slavery in South. (North kept slavery in Northern territory; also, hard-core abolitionists supported both Southern secession and abolition of slavery as same issue of freedom.)

Spanish-American War — U.S. interests grabbed Spanish colonies (Cuba, Philippines) for exploitation and turned the U.S. State into an old-world empire. **Pretext:** U.S. battleship *Maine* was "attacked" in a Cuban harbor. (Even though innocent, Spain apologized anyway and bent over backwards to avoid war.)

World War I — U.S. interests, especially bankers, bet on Great Britain and moved U.S. in to save their investments when Russians pulled out leaving Germany one front. **Pretext:** German U-Boats attacked *British* ship carrying Americans; declaration of unrestricted submarine warfare zones by Germany. (Trivial relative to war, and U.S. ships should have "taken their chances" if they insisted on running huge risks for high profits by penetrating the blockades. GB was blockading Germany and other interests wanted to replay "War of 1812" and attack *Britain*.)

World War II (Europe, 1939) — Britain gave Poland a "blank-check treaty" if they would hold out 99%-German Danzig from Germany — the last adjustment of the Versailles Treaty (ending WWI) that penalized Germany. Also, Britain and France refused alliance with Russia against the "fascist menace" (although Bolshevik Russia *was* seriously threatened by Nazi aggression, unlike Danzig-less Poland, not to mention distant Great Britain) and thus pushed USSR to German side in fear. Poland was overwhelmingly outnumbered and still refused to return German Danzig. **Pretext:** Germany invaded Poland without provocation. (Nonsense; allied war propaganda. Poland was so surprised that they were already fully mobilized and standing on the border on September 1, 1939.)

World War II (Pacific, 1941) — The United States New Deal administration sought entry to the European theatre (above) and required an "attack" since 80% of Americans opposed "bailing out Britain" again. Japanese were strangled by British blockade aided by "neutral" U.S. ships; Japanese funds in U.S. were seized by U.S. government, and Japanese emissaries for peace were insulted and scorned. **Pretext:** Japan attacked Pearl Harbor naval installation — few, if any *innocent* U.S. civilians injured. (Japan knew it would be dragged into the war and would lose; it struck first to delay the inevitable. Japanese "bushido" code was offended — deliberately and provocatively — by U.S. statists.)

Korean War — Artificial division of Korea (WWII) between a Northern communist dictatorship and a Southern, pro-U.S. State dictatorship; U.S. entered to prop up colonies France and Japan were abandoning in Southeast Asia for variety of corporate-interest and Soviet-containment reasons. **Pretext:** Communist aggression which involved China and Russia. (China attacked the U.S. *after* American troops threatened to cross the Yalu River into China. Russia sat back and sold arms — as the U.S. had done *before* landing troops.)

Vietnam War — U.S. attempted to keep former French Indo-China from passing into Eastern bloc. (See Korean War; this was a continuation from 1954.) As became obvious immediately after, when China switched over to U.S. side, "Communist" countries are not *necessarily* threats to U.S. **Pretext:** Defend South Vietnamese, who wanted Western-style democracy, from Communist form of statists. (South Vietnamese were split and there was never anything even as "free" as democracy there under the various generals and the Diem dictatorship.)

El Salvador — Certain U.S. industries and banks have heavy investments in Latin American countries and fear their expropriation by Communist or Marxist governments. **Pretext:** Salvadorans want democracy, not communism. (Salvadorans voted in U.S.-monitored election and *got* a genuine fascist government [ARENA party of Roberto D'Aubuisson] and massive murder of "democrats" — let alone communists — by ARENA death squads. The U.S. then overruled the results of an election they had demanded in the first place.)

Iraq War I — U.S. sought to preserve its interests in Saudi Arabian oil fields, fearing that if Kuwait fell and former U.S. ally Saddam Hussein enriched himself from oil profits there, then Saudi Arabia might be next. **Pretext:** Iraq invaded Kuwait (separated from Iraq by British in 1932) to regain its port and to seize oil fields on the theory that they were using a slant drill to "drink the milkshake" of Iraq's al-Rumaila fields.

Afghan War — U.S. and U.K. attempt to secure Afghanistan to protect a proposed natural gas pipeline from Turkmenistan to Pakistan and India passing right through the Kandahar province. This, in an effort to counteract perceived Russo-Iranian energy trade in the region. **Pretext:** Taliban gave aid and comfort to 9/11 attack coordinator Osama bin Laden, oppressed women, and served as a training haven for Islamic fundamentalist terrorists.

Iraq War II — U.S. continued to perceive Iraq as a threat to its oil interests in the middle east, especially after Iraq's scorched-earth retreat from the Kuwaiti oil fields in 1991. In addition, personal grudges may have played a part, since the sitting president's father had once been targeted for assassination by Hussein. **Pretext:** Saddam Hussein's repeated scofflawing of numerous U.N. resolutions and rumours that Iraq still pursued weapons of mass destruction.

By the way, those quickie explanations are not meant to convince you that the U.S. was wrong and the other sides were right. The agorist viewpoint is that *the U.S. State was wrong* and *its war opponents were wrong*. Both or either could have avoided any of the above wars.

And, before we forget, there is an obvious third way the North American non-state defends itself against the State around it, if it is agorist. The protection agencies form larger *syndicates* than the ones they form in the case we mentioned above of a local protection company going renegade. If *all* the policy holders of all the insurance and protection companies are threatened by invasion, they will throw all their combined resources (and higher technology, judging by free enterprise's past performance) on defence of the common ground.

Fourth, the people would rise up in militias or guerrilla units to defend their incredibly free society. (There were advance hints of this strategy when the Ukrainian Anarchist army, under Nestor Makhno, had no trouble raising militia to protect the local fanners from roving armies of Reds and Whites during the Russian Revolution.)

Fifth, most wars have had a strong Economic component. Often access to goods or natural resources was barred by protectionist State Economic policies. The anarchy would have full free trade with full access. Anyone wanting anything produced in the North American anarchy could easily *buy* it —without taxes and tariffs and at a cheaper price than anywhere else. (Notice how giant Communist China went out of its way not to conquer tiny Hong Kong, although the British were ready to toss it to them any time they asked, and finally did. Even now, Hong Kong has not seen Red Chinese tanks rolling through its streets to crush its capitalist minions. In fact, much of China has become a *mirror* of Hong Kong, with Party leaders and the People's Liberation Army growing rich on market activities white, black, and grey. Check also the little free ports and cities of Monaco, Andorra, Liechtenstein, Singapore and San Marino.)

Sixth, (and we'll have to stop eventually, so let it be here) the States will quarrel amongst themselves. Since the anarchy threatens no State immediately (point two) (long-term, it does, as a shining example of better conditions), but other States with standing militaries do threaten at all times, what State would want the easy-access to resources (point five) in the anarchy cut off by another State using it? That could mean *war* — but among the States while the Anarchy freely sells to all sides without favor or penalty.

Critics of market anarchy often try to have their cake and eat it too. For example, they may argue that there are too few States — "what happens if the States gang up?" — and at the same time too many — "how can one anarchy survive among all those States?" As in the case of historical examples such as Revolutionary France and Revolutionary Russia where the surrounding States did gang up to crush the new type of State, if the country is big enough, it will survive even foreign interference, even in the middle of civil war (which both experienced) — let alone agorist peace.

Additional tactics for defence and reasons for nonaggression are left as an exercise for the reader.

The Agorist Path

Getting from here (statism) to there (agorism) is the second and perhaps defining characteristic of the latter. Unlike libertarianism, agorism offers both *goal* and *path* as an internally consistent package deal.

The short answer is given in Axiom Four. A longer answer is *"applying Counter-Economics to all your actions and linking preferentially with others who do so creates an ever-bigger agora."* How that works — and what two things you need to watch for — is an excellent chapter with which to end this primer.

Chapter Eight
APPLIED AGORISM

At this concluding point, we would like to tie together all we have learned. Thus we can see clearly the path to be taken with a view to ending up with a new ability: to figure out how each of us can best walk that path to our own advantage. So let us begin by visualizing that pathway.

The Road From Agora

Since we have some picture of an agorist society and an all-too-good picture of a statist society, let us connect them by slowly degenerating one into the other. Since it is usually more difficult to see how the "real here-and-now" becomes the possible, let's run the film backwards. Let us start with an agorist society and run backwards in time to what we have now, a statist society.

The State exists because of a mystique that confers upon it the sanction of the victim. Thus, we each must have lost our sanction of the State for the agora to have come about. Very well, running the film of this in-between period backward, it should appear that some "mental plague" is infecting contented agorists to persuade them, one by one, to give up their freedom and submit to control by some embryonic government (a criminal gang with a good line of buncombe).

At first the State would be able to tax and mobilize only its followers. It would be a voluntary organization — sadomasochistic, to be sure, but still tolerated by the unaffected agorists. Every time the State tried to prey on insured agorists, it would be brought to arbitration and restitution enforced.

Still, against all reason, the infection grows and the State is too powerful now for restitution to be enforced. Some privileged people are able to live successfully off plunder and be protected by the mindless subjects of the new State who will sacrifice their own property, and even their lives, so that some may live off others. (Remember, this is the opposite of how people think sanely because we are deliberately going backwards. It should be a comfort to know that this route is *highly* unlikely in a forward direction.)

The State now has its power elite, ruling class, conspiracy, or whatever term you like best. They can distribute some of this unearned wealth to bribe agorists who have little conviction (and a weak will) to join the infected masses. Now the State reaches a level that permits it not only to stave off the protection companies, but actually to attack them. At this point, the companies go "underground" or Counter-Economic, still enforcing contracts among the remaining agorists and those who are not being very well defended by the inefficient State apparatus, as well as those who are not in favor with the Statists' top-level elite. Otherwise, people look out for Statist enforcers as much as possible and develop evasive techniques in order to keep their manufacture, trade and services from detection and capture. They develop Counter-Economic techniques. And they keep on going.

Finally, the State compels its new citizens to give up their gold for worthless paper; and then the State divides into several States and mobilizes the citizens to get to see which ruling class will get the biggest share of the tax plunder. Sound like we've gone a little crazy in imagining anyone permitting this? True enough, but unfortunately, this craziest picture of all describes nothing less than the reality we live in right now.

The path from here to agora now becomes blindingly obvious. As more people reject the State's mystifications — nationalism, pseudo-Economics, false threats, and betrayed political promises — the Counter-Economy grows both vertically and horizontally. Horizontally, it involves more and more people who turn more and more of their activities toward the counter-economic; vertically, it means new structures (businesses and services) grow specifically to serve the Counter-Economy (safe communication links, arbitrators, insurance for specifically "illegal" activities, early forms of protection technology, and even guards and protectors). Eventually, the "underground" breaks into the overground where most people are agorists, few are statists, and the nearest State enforcement cannot effectively crush them.

These *agorist condensations* are highly vulnerable when first exposed but will probably evaporate back into the anonymous masses when seriously threatened. Finally, one grows large enough to defend itself against the nearest State (see Chapter Seven regarding the many ways that it can defend itself). Others rally to it and those agorists staying "home" under States' rule become ever-richer trading ports with the first agora condensations.

The rapid collapse of State taxation ability at this point will push the State to rely even more on inflation to support itself. The Counter-Economists abandon fiat money ever-faster and use gold and trusted agorist gold warehouse receipts ("hard-money cheques"). The runaway inflation approaches what Ludwig Von Mises termed "the Crack-Up Boom," paper money is completely abandoned, like 1923 German *reichsmarks* and 1781 U.S. Continentals and 1787 French *assignats*. (See the aforementioned novel *Alongside Night* for a thrilling presentation of this scenario.)

At the critical point when the protection companies can protect anyone who asks for a policy and is willing to pay for it, the State loses its monopoly of legitimized coercion. Once the power elite realizes that "it has come to this," they will throw all the force they have left at the agora. The protection companies will defend the agorists, the taxpayers will flee the State to the free market, the military will desert as the State runs out of (acceptable) pay and supplies for them, and the State will collapse. (The last sentence describes the Agorist Revolution, accept no substitute behavior involving agorist "attacks" on the State. We are strictly defensive. Some people with grudges against the State, incited because of State-murdered loved ones, may undertake some spectacular commando raids and such, but that would not be the norm.)

Having spelled all this out, we still have one big question left unanswered: why has this not happened already?

The False Dichotomy

Divide and conquer has been a statist motto and tactic since Julius Cæsar. The division of libertarianism from Counter-Economics has many causes but several can be attributed to Statist encouragement of illogic, irrationality, and sheer mysticism. Nowhere is this more evident than in the very field of thought confronting us: moral philosophy and economics. (It is noteworthy here to remember that the first economist, Adam Smith, was a professor of Moral Philosophy.)

Morally, the State and its clerical toadies have separated the moral from the practical. Several strains of religious thought, Kantian altruism, down to Hegel's explicit worship of the State, have told people to try to live morally, but always fail; then the people were to let the State (with the blessings of the Established Church of Statist ideology) punish them.

Economically, the Court Economists have distorted and changed the laws of economics to suit the ruling group. Mercantilism, economic nationalism, Fabianism, fascism, Keynsianism, monetarism, supply-side Economics, socialism, social democracy, progressivism, New Deal, Fair Deal, Square Deal, New Frontier, Just Society, Great Society, war communism, unspecified Hope and Change, and middle-of-the-road-ism are political frauds and economic nonsense. In most cases, the priests, intellectuals, and rulers knew what they were doing and continued doing it until the snake oil no longer sold. Then they simply slapped a new label on the same noxious brew.

Most people are ignorant of economics today and remain frightened by the subject. Most people think morality is either impossible, irrelevant, or something they can do nothing about but which will catch up with them eventually, either while they are alive or after their death. As many sages have repeated, the truth will set you free. Even the cases where the truth was dimly seen "as through a glass darkly," the liberating effects have been visible. Rebellious religious sects often morphed into authoritarian cults, but some achieved incredible freedom, such as the Rhode Island Baptists, the Pennsylvanian Quakers, and the American Deists, who advanced the American Revolutionary ideology. Adam Smith and his immediate followers in Europe created such an impact in the early 19th Century trade policies that a wave of economic prosperity swept the world with just a lowering of trade barriers toward freedom.

Then came World War I and the heyday of socialism, justified largely by the "failure" of free
enterprise. (It did not fail, it was stifled by internal
"progressive" regulation and external war "emer-
gencies.") With the collapse of socialism and its
various offspring such as Soviet Communism and
American Liberalism, a vacuum has opened for
an ideology to inspire and guide thinking people.
Though the States of the world give lip-service to
various socialist ideals, they are aware (or their
Higher Circles are aware) that socialist ideals are
losing their ability to beguile. Perhaps something
called Libertarianism, having given up its remaining ties to Liberty while promising to provide it
through Statism, will be the next bottle of snake
oil the confidence men of the State will offer to
maintain our sanctions.

The State in the Mind

The State has guns and men to use them. As
we have seen, however, it not only can fail to
coerce a rebellious *majority*, it cannot even stop
an enterprising *minority* of black marketeers
and other Counter-Economists. The State must
be defeated in each person's *mind*. Once you personally reject its hold over you, you are as free as
your intelligence, your will to take risks, and the
aid of your allies can keep you. New converts to
Christianity describe a similar process, which they
call being "born again." Even in darkest Russia
or China, entrepreneurs thrive and — for a high

price — buy their well-being and additional freedom. Of course, any North American, Australian, or European reading this should have a relatively easier time and a higher payoff.

What may be needed — in addition to spreading the word and living it — is some form of agorist psychology. Perhaps we can use the examples of therapy for childhood mistreatment or consciousness-raising groups for feminists, gays, and other obviously oppressed groups. We can all get together in small affinity groups of trusted friends and allies to dig our contradictions out of our unconscious. We can flush out the State from our heads by ourselves or together or both ways.

Every law that you obey must be reexamined with the thought, *how does it protect life and property?* If, as almost every law in our system does, it actually *constricts* the market or *steals* outright, it should not be obeyed save when force is reported nearby and menacing you directly.

Once you have successfully arranged your life to live in the free-market anarchy to the extent that you can accept the risks — the higher the risks, the bigger the payoff, including freedom — you can and will quite naturally add to your ranks. Risks are lowered by trustworthy marketeers working together. Soon everyone will know agorists are the most trustworthy of all. Come runaway inflation and depressions, the unemployed and bankrupt in the State's Economy will see unlimited jobs and entrepreneurial opportunities, not to mention the preserved wealth for capital, that the Counter-

Economy offers and join it if only to keep from starving, losing their homes, their family support, and their remaining self-respect.

Remember, an agorist is one who lives counter-economically without guilt for his or her heroic, day-to-day actions, with the old libertarian morality of never violating another's person or property. There is no "membership card" to fool you; an agorist is one who lives agorism. Accept no counterfeits.

There are agorists "trying to live up to it." There are, of course, liars who will claim to be anything. As Yoda said so succinctly, "*Do*. Or do not. There is no *try*."

That's Agorism.

AFTERWORD

Beyond Basic Agorism

A few words may be appropriate here for the reader who enjoyed the primer but wishes to go on to the hard stuff. There are two ways to go.

Horizontally, one can delve deeply into economics, Counter-Economics, Revisionist History, and some areas not really covered here, such as libertarian philosophy, psychology, and literature. There are plenty of sources for those who wish to check out some of our claims here or specialize in an area of personal excitement.

Vertically, one has fewer choices because few publications have emerged so far from this brand-new movement. This author has published *New Libertarian Manifesto* — available from KoPubCo — for those who wish to go beyond mere simple agorism to become activists, advance protection agents defending the Counter-Economy by public relations, education... and other means.

Websites, such as agorism.info and agorist.com, have sprung up, created by agorists eager to extend theory into practical action.

An Agorist Primer

A full-sized book — *Counter-Economics* — is awaiting publication at KoPubCo, [*though it lay unfinished at the time of SEK3's death. —VK*]. It will emphasize examples and practice, the theory being as much as already covered here.

This paperback edition of *An Agorist Primer* is set in Century Schoolbook type, a very pleasant and readable font, at 12 points on 14 point leading. Titles are in Academy Engraved and Baskerville Old Face. Typesetting, layout, and cover design was performed by Black Dawn Graphics, which has provided services to KoPubCo since 1983.

About the Author

Samuel Edward Konkin III was a vanguard movement theorist and hard-core activist since the historic split between libertarians and conservatives at the YAF convention in St. Louis, 1969. In the subsequent three and a half decades, he served as editor and publisher of the longest-lived libertarian publication, beginning as *Laissez-Faire!* (1970), then as *New Libertarian Notes* (1971-75), *New Libertarian Weekly* (1975-77, the longest-running libertarian weekly), and *New Libertarian* (1978-1990). He wrote the seminal work on agorism, *New Libertarian Manifesto*, in 1980.

He has coined the following terms and concepts, many of which have turned up in all libertarian publications: Counter-Economics, agorism, minarchy, partyarchy, anti-principles, Left Libertarianism, anarchozionism, "Browne-out," red market, Kochtopus, and more. He has influenced the works of authors such as J. Neil Schulman (*Alongside Night*) and Victor Koman (*Solomon's Knife*), who both had their first professional fiction sales in the pages of his publications.

Mr. Konkin served as Executive Director of the Agorist Institute, an outreach organization promulgating the principles of agorism and counter-economics. He was guest of honor at science-fiction conventions and libertarian gatherings and was a seasoned world traveller. His unfinished *magnum opus, Counter-Economics*, will see publication in the near future.

Mr. Konkin died February 23, 2004.

NEW
LIBERTARIAN
MANIFESTO

The classic of libertarian theory and practice is back in print in a newly re-typeset, pocket-sized edition! One of the most influential works in the field, *New Libertarian Manifesto* is more timely than ever. Includes critiques by Murray N. Rothbard, Robert LeFevre, and Erwin S. "Filthy Pierre" Strauss, and responses by Samuel Edward Konkin III.

"Konkin's writings are to be welcomed. Because we need a lot more poly-centrism in the movement. Because he shakes up Partyarchs who tend to fall into unthinking compla-cency. And especially because he cares deeply about liberty and can read and write, qualities which seem to be going out of style in the libertarian movement."
—Murray N. Rothbard, Ph.D.

www.kopubco.com/nlm.html
ISBN 978-0-9777649-2-1

KoPubCo is the publishing division of
The Triplanetary Corporation

AN AGORIST PRIMER

The Hardcover Keepsake First Edition

You've read this modern classic of agorist theory and practice by Samuel Edward Konkin III in its paperback version, but if you want to read it again and again or give it as a cherished gift, copies of the hardcover first edition are available from the publisher or Amazon.com.

"A lot of us have waited two decades for the release of this slender tome.... Clocking in at just over 100 pages, *An Agorist Primer* offers not only a simple-but-thorough explanation of what agorism is, it also builds a rock-solid case for it.... But trust me, Konkin's well-structured argument for a free society of the open marketplace... is compelling. And he shows convincingly that such a society is absolutely achievable and sustainable.

"Sam's book truly is a primer; he strips down heavy-duty economic theory and libertarian philosophy without diminishing either of them. *An Agorist Primer* may be a quick walk through the basics, but it never shortchanges the reader. And best of all, it's awfully entertaining."

—Wally Conger, *Out of Step*

www.kopubco.com/aap_hb.html
ISBN 978-0-9777649-4-5

KoPubCo is the publishing division of
The Triplanetary Corporation

CPSIA information can be obtained at www.ICGtesting.com
Printed in the USA
LVOW11s1106210216

476055LV00001B/130/P